GIANTS OF THE ROAD

THE HISTORY OF LAND TRANSPORTATION

David Jefferis

Franklin Watts
New York   London   Toronto   Sydney

Illustrated by
Robert Burns
Chris Forsey
Ron Jobson
Michael Roffe

Photographs supplied by
Mary Evans Picture Library
David Jefferis
Roger Levy
Jerry Mason
Truck Magazine

Technical consultant
Patrick Devereux

© 1991 Franklin Watts

Franklin Watts Inc.
387 Park Avenue South
New York, NY 10016

Printed in Belgium

Library of Congress Cataloging-in-Publication Data

Jefferis, David
Giants of the road : the history of trucks / David Jefferis.
p. cm – – (Wheels)
Summary: Presents the development of trucks with information
on different kinds of trucks and their purposes.
ISBN 0–531–14123–3
1. Trucks – Juvenile literature.
[1. Trucks.] I. Title. II. Series: Wheels.
TL230.15.L34 1991
629.224 – dc20

90-31659
CIP AC

GIANTS OF THE ROAD

Contents

Introduction	4
The first trucks	6
Improving the breed	8
Bigger and bigger	10
Military trucks	12
Highway express	14
Long-distance trucking	16
Heavy loads	18
Mining giants	20
Wreck and recovery	22
Future trucks	24
Trucking progress	26
Facts and records	28
Truck technology	30
Index	32

Introduction

In today's world, the truck is king of the transportation business. But it wasn't always like that. The earliest trucks were unreliable contraptions, powered by primitive steam engines. In the 18th century, several inventors designed and built such machines. In 1769 Frenchman Nicolas Cugnot demonstrated his three-wheeled artillery tractor to the French Army. The vehicle proved no competitor to the horses and oxen that were used to pull guns at the time, but it scored an important first as the first practical self-propelled vehicle ever made.

Since the days of the first trucks, more and more of the world's cargo has been carried on the roads. Up to the 1950s though, railroad trains carried most bulk freight, while trucks provided door-to-door transportation at either end of each rail journey. But since then, many long-distance highways have been built, allowing truckers to drive at high speeds for hours at a time. So today it usually makes more sense to send freight the whole way by road. This avoids having to transfer loads on and off trains, and it saves freight operators time and money.

The success of the truck industry has brought some of its own problems however. Large and heavy vehicles create noise, vibration and traffic congestion. Many people suffer these every day if they live near a busy highway. For others, a bypass road can be an expensive solution. In the future it is likely that governments may encourage the return of at least some freight back to the railroads.

◁ Almost every cargo is carried by truck at some stage in its journey. Here, lines of trucks wait at a ferry terminal for a ship to take them overseas. Trucks like these often carry containers. These are standard-size metal "shoe boxes", filled with cargo.

Trucks old and new

These two highway giants cover a period of more than 90 years. During this time, truck design and performance have improved enormously. The earliest trucks had open cabs, solid tires and primitive engines. Today's trucks are comfortable, reliable and can cruise at high speeds.

1898 Daimler

Starting handle

◁ The 1898 Daimler from Germany had a front-mounted engine and a padded seat for the driver. To start the engine, you had to turn the starting handle in front of the truck. Cranking an unreliable engine into action was hard work, but it was probably a good way to warm up on a cold morning! The Daimler's wooden spoke wheels had tires of solid rubber.

▽ The 1990 Iveco-Ford Turbostar is typical of the latest generation of high-speed haulers, able to maintain cruising speeds of 100 km/h (62 mph) or more with ease. The powerful engine is mounted under the driving cab.

1990 Iveco-Ford

The first trucks

Safety was a major concern for the steam truck inventors of the 19th century. People were used to the gentle pace of animal transportation, and the new machines were prone to steering failures and boiler explosions, which did little to calm public suspicion. But the 1827 steam carriage designed by Englishman Goldsworthy Gurney attempted to answer some of the problems. It had a boiler with a safety valve and a furnace that used clean-burning coke instead of dirty, smelly coal. By 1831, Gurney's carriages were making regular runs, at speeds of over 20 km/h (13 mph). But there was much opposition to steam on the roads and with the coming of the railroads, there wasn't much support for other types of steam transportation on land. The truck had to wait for a better engine to be developed.

In 1885, German engineer Karl Benz put the finishing touches to his new creation. This was a three-wheeled motor carriage, powered by the new internal-combustion engine, based on the ideas of another German, Nicolaus Otto. Its fuel was burned inside a cylinder, and power was produced by the back and forth movement of a piston in the cylinder. The new engine was far more powerful for its weight than a steam engine. And the fuel was gasoline, which was a lot easier to handle than lumps of coal. It could be poured straight into a fuel tank, a simple process.

When the first cars proved successful, "horseless carriage fever" swept through Europe and the United States. And together with plans for faster and better automobiles, inventors rushed to develop bigger vehicles as load carriers to replace the horse and cart. One of the first trucks to go into production was the Langert wagon, made by a company based in Philadelphia, Pennsylvania. In Europe, the first truck was a German Daimler, which weighed two tons.

◁ Cugnot's artillery tractor. The huge copper boiler provided steam for the piston, which was mounted by the front wheel.

△ A stoker clung precariously to the rear platform on Gurney's steam carriage, while shoveling coke into the furnace. Driver and passengers sat up front, away from the heat and fumes.

△ Steam traction engines provided reliable service for many years. They had various uses – this one is operating as a crane, lifting a gun barrel onto its carriage.

▷ Later steamers included this small, wooden Thornycroft. Heavy steamers were built as late as the 1920s. The six-ton Foden, shown far right, was built for beer deliveries in 1929.

Improving the breed

Most of today's trucks are powered by diesel engines. But at the beginning of this century, there was no general rule. The choice offered by truck manufacturers covered a wide range of engines, including ones running on steam, gasoline, kerosene oil and electricity. Steam trucks were popular, particularly in places where coal was cheap. Electricity was ideal for local deliveries in towns and cities, with loads such as milk and groceries. The problem with the early internal-combustion engines was reliability. Rather than having deliveries stopped by breakdowns, most firms preferred older but more reliable means of transportation, such as horses or steam trucks.

World War I marked a turning point in truck design. The first military trucks suffered many problems. The thick mud of the battlefront in France soon had vehicles sinking up to their axles. And bad weather revealed the poor reliability of the electrical systems and other major components. But new trucks were soon designed to cope with the rough conditions. One of the first was the American Mack AC, nicknamed the "bulldog" for its blunt nose and toughness. This nickname was so widely used that Mack adopted the bulldog for its emblem, and it still uses it today.

When the war ended, the strength and reliability of the Mack and trucks like it proved useful in the commercial world. Other developments, such as windows and electric lights, came from passenger cars. On lighter trucks, air-filled pneumatic tires were a new idea.

△ The Mack AC was nicknamed the "bulldog" by British troops. Under the blunt nose, the engine was connected to the rear wheels by a drive chain. Like many other trucks of its time, the Mack had a set of puncture-proof solid rubber tires.

△ Electric trucks were quiet and economical over short distances. The Walker electric truck shown here was made in 1919 for a luxury London store. It could go up to 96 km (60 miles) on its Edison nickel iron batteries before they needed recharging.

△ ▷ Truck tires went through several stages of development. The first tires were made of metal, as shown here on a World War I German army truck. Spare tire sections were carried above the rear wheels. Some were fitted with big spikes for better grip on muddy tracks. Solid rubber tires came next, and only after the war did pneumatic, air-filled rubber tires come into widespread use. Today all tires use the pneumatic design, which gives a smooth, cushioned ride even over rough surfaces.

Metal tire   Solid rubber tire   Pneumatic tire

Trucks of the world

Here are the medallions of some well-known truck manufacturers. In recent years, many firms have joined forces. Leyland of Great Britain, for example, now makes trucks with the DAF truck group from Holland.

Bigger and bigger

△ The Scammell Pioneer was a very successful early articulated design.

After World War I, thousands of old army trucks were sold off to civil buyers for use as road transportation. The new pneumatic tires caused problems as loads got bigger. The extra weight made them prone to punctures and caused damage to soft-surfaced roads. So truck designers added extra wheels to take the strain. Two wheels at the front for steering with four at the back to spread the weight more evenly on the road were common.

The first semitrucks went into service in the 1920s. Using a tractor section in front to pull a separate load had two major advantages. It was more maneuverable than a rigid design of the same length, so it could tackle tight corners more easily. Also, the cargo section could be unhitched for loading, while the tractor part was used for another job.

Diesel power really took off in the 1930s. In this period, much of the world was in the grip of the Depression. Millions of people were out of work and many firms had to cut costs to stay in business. The diesel's main advantage was its economy. It used far less fuel than a gasoline engine of the same size, so many trucks went over to diesel power. The diesel engine has never looked back, and today almost all heavy trucks use this type of engine. The exception for a while was the United States which didn't really turn to diesel power until much later. Cheap home-produced gasoline meant that fuel economy was not so important there as it was in other countries where imported fuel was increasingly expensive. Vehicle economy became important in the United States when it began importing fuel in the 1960s.

Rigids and semis

There are two main types of trucks, rigid and semi. Smaller trucks are mostly of rigid design. The vehicle is one unit, with the engine, cab and load area mounted on a single chassis. Big trucks are usually semis, with a joint in the middle so they can be manoeuvred easily. The tractor unit at the front tows a semitrailer. A trailer has front wheels and a drawbar. Jackknifing is a danger with semis on slippery roads, and many new trucks have antilock brakes to prevent this.

Rigid vehicle

Semi vehicle

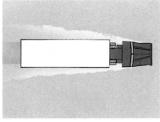 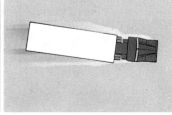 

1 Semitruck traveling on a wet road starts to brake.

2 Wheels skid, semitrailer starts to snake sideways.

3 Semitrailer pushes forward and vehicle slides into a jackknife.

▽ Rocketlike shapes were styling themes in the 1930s. This White semi looks ready for the launch pad, but in fact, the 1937 truck hauled beer for a Canadian brewery.

Military trucks

In World War II, military trucks were as essential to fighting forces as tanks and aircraft. Germany's lightning attacks in 1939 and 1940 were successful largely because they were motorized; their speed took their victims by surprise. First of all, aircraft "softened up" targets by bombing them, then tanks and armored cars were used to spearhead the land attack. Support troops and essential supplies such as ammunition, food and fuel, came up in the rear, transported by heavy-duty trucks. Without these basic materials, the attacks would soon have come to a grinding halt.

Off-road driving was essential in wartime, as roads were often bombed or impassable. To get across rough country, many trucks had 4-wheel drive. If one tire lost grip and spun in the mud, then others were available to pull the vehicle out of trouble. During the war, truck production was far greater than in peacetime. These fighting vehicles were so toughly built that many survive today, often working as wrecker trucks, or on other off-road tasks.

Today's military trucks include highly specialized vehicles such as missile carriers and tank transporters, as well as more conventional-looking troop and cargo haulers. These are often based on civilian models, but with stronger components fitted where necessary to bring them up to military specification. Multi-purpose vehicles are popular too, as it is cheaper to modify one basic design than to produce a new design for each separate task.

▽ Two military semitrucks. Top, a 1943 Reo aircraft refueling tanker. Bottom, a Minuteman missile carrier from the 1960s. Housed in its metal container, a Minuteman missile could be transported anywhere, by road or by cargo plane.

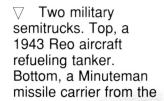

▷ A number code system indicates how many wheels a truck has. The code is used for all trucks, civil or military. It also shows which wheels are powered. The number of tires on each axle is not recorded.

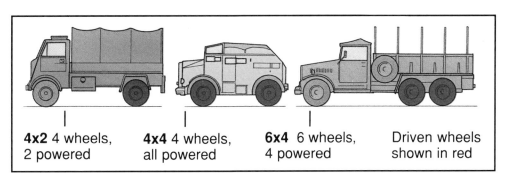

4x2 4 wheels, 2 powered   **4x4** 4 wheels, all powered   **6x4** 6 wheels, 4 powered   Driven wheels shown in red

▷ Common to most military vehicles are a tough construction and high ground clearance to give mobility on and near the battlefield.

▽ Tank transporters are military truck giants. This one weighs 89 tons, including a 62-ton tank. It can haul its load at up to 70 km/h (44 mph). The newest trucks have a modular, "building block," construction, which allows spare parts to be slotted in easily when needed.

Highway Express

The most popular type of truck for hauling big loads is now the semitruck vehicle. A powerful tractor unit hauls a semitrailer, which can weigh 38 tons or more when loaded. The maximum weight allowed varies from country to country. Tractors can be of conventional design, with the engine under a front hood, or cab-over, with the engine under the driving cab. An advantage of the cab-over design is that the tractor can be shorter than the conventional unit. This allows longer semitrailers to be attached in those countries that have vehicle length limits.

One of the most advanced conventional units is the American Kenworth T600 Aerodyne, nicknamed the "Anteater" for its long curving nose. Running a truck such as this is not cheap: with extras, it can cost $150,000 or more to buy. On the road, the rig (the complete tractor and semitrailer unit) consumes diesel fuel at a rate of about 3 km per liter (8.5 miles per gallon). Added to the purchase and fuel costs are essential items such as insurance, maintenance and the driver's pay. Truck owners work their vehicles hard to make them earn their keep as they make money only when on the move. A distance of 160,000 km (100,000 miles) a year is quite normal.

For long-distance work that includes overnight stops, many truckers have sleeper cabs on their rigs. With a sleeper cab a driver can get a comfortable night's rest, without having to pay for a hotel. Typical items in a sleeper cab include a small refrigerator, stereo system, microwave oven, television and a bunk bed.

▷ The Kenworth Aerodyne is more streamlined than many conventional tractors, which results in up to 22 per cent better fuel consumption. Special bodied versions are also available to smooth the flowing lines still more. To keep in touch with base, many trucks have two-way radios. Over 10,000 truckers in the United States use satellite systems to talk over long distances.

△ A trucker spends a lot of time in the cab, so it should be a comfortable place to work in. Seats are fully adjustable. Steering and other controls are power assisted. Big windows and rear-view mirrors provide good visibility for safe driving.

▽ This White Freightliner is a cab-over truck made in the United States. Twin rear wheels, tall exhaust pipes and roof-mounted warning horns are typical features. Extra marker lights for safe night running are popular items too.

Long-distance trucking

The construction of major highways across the world has given the truck industry a huge boost. Today trucks compete successfully with the railroads on all overland routes, even those that involve time-consuming border crossings between countries.

In Europe such transcontinental haulers display TIR signs on their rigs. TIR stands for Transports Internationaux Routiers, and *routier* is French for truck driver. Many TIR trucks haul loads packed in containers. These are standard-size metal boxes that can be carried on trucks, trains and cargo ships. They are used for traveling between countries because they are sealed after loading. At each border point, customs officials inspect the official seals to check that no one has tampered with them – whether to steal the load or to smuggle goods, such as diamonds or drugs. If the seals have been broken, customs officers can check inside the containers. Otherwise they will let them through, making such border crossings mostly quick and easy.

▽ Long-distance hauling across Australia. The route shown here includes busy highways and dusty tracks.

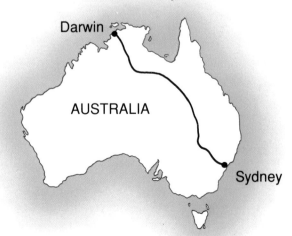

Some countries, such as the United States and Australia, are big enough for long-distance runs without any border crossings. A typical marathon journey in Australia runs from Sydney in the east to Darwin in the north, a distance of over 4,000 km (2,500 miles). Once clear of the eastern section, trailers are added to make a trucking oddity, the Australian roadtrain. With three trailers bucking behind in the outback dust, a roadtrain driver may be in charge of 130 tons of cargo. Big fuel tanks go with the long distances: a fill-up of 450 liters (99 gallons) of diesel is typical, which is enough to go nearly 1,120 km (700 miles) before the next fuel stop. Towards Darwin, noon temperatures can climb over 40°C (104°F), so truckers keep daytime speeds down to around 70 km/h (44 mph) to avoid overheating the tires. At night, Australia's wildlife is a danger. Kangaroos hop across the dirt roads, with little regard for what's coming towards them. Every roadtrain has a set of steel "roo bars" on the front to protect the truck from collision damage.

◁ Australian roadtrains have steel "roo bars" to fend off the kangaroos that sometimes leap in front of approaching vehicles.

▽ European truck journeys often stretch over similar distances to those in Australia and the United States. A typical long-distance journey includes several border crossings, as many European countries are quite small.

△ Swedish Volvo trucks are widely used.

△ A Pegaso Troner from Spain.

Heavy loads

△ Hauling huge loads was all in a day's work for the sturdy 1929 Scammell tractor.

One of the first really big trucks was the 1929 Scammell. Before this, it often took three or four steam tractors to transport super-heavy loads. Now a single Scammell could pull 100 tons at a time. The powerful truck's big engine guzzled fuel, but steamer crews had to fill up with water about every 32 km (20 miles), and the Scammell had a much longer range than this. The second 100-ton Scammell was named *Leaping Lena*, for the way its front wheels left the ground when the truck strained against a big load. One of the problems for Lena's drivers was the way she regularly sank into the soft roads, which were not made to support such weights. To get around tight corners, a steersman at the back of the rig received orders from the driver by telephone, turning the rear wheels as directed. Later Scammells continued the

tradition of heavy haulage. In 1977, a Scammell pulled a 634-ton load for 40 km (25 miles).

Among the big haulers in service today are the American Darts used to carry salt in Mexico. Each huge Dart rig is nearly 61 metres (200 ft) long, and takes a load of 360 tons of salt. The salt is mostly exported from Mexico to Japan, where it is used in chemical production. Salt is highly corrosive, so the Darts are specially equipped to combat rust, with stainless steel fittings and many coats of zinc paint. They are also made from a special type of corrosion-resistant steel.

Once loaded up, the Darts move quickly for their size. Roaring along at over 50 km/h (31 mph), they take the salt to the nearest harbor where it is loaded aboard waiting cargo ships. Next stop, Japan!

△ A Kenworth tractor-trailer rig was used to haul this Space Shuttle Orbiter from the assembly plant in 1979. Though the Orbiter is over 37 m (122 ft) long, it is no record breaker so far as giant loads go. The biggest load ever hauled was a Dutch oil rig in 1984. It weighed nearly 4,000 tons.

▷ A Dart rig being loaded with salt. To keep rust at bay, salt crystals are washed off at the end of each day's work. The Dart company dates from 1903, the same as the better-known Ford Motor Company.

Mining giants

Dump trucks are among the largest vehicles and are used by the mining and construction industries for carrying big loads. The Lectra Haul is popular for such work. The M100 model weighs 65 tons and can carry a load of up to 100 tons at a time in its massive steel cargo bay. This sounds like a lot, and it is: the weight is about the same as a stack of 50 large cars. The Lectra Haul's power comes from a mighty Cummins diesel engine, which charges two powerful electric motors, one for each back wheel. When the truck goes downhill, the electric motors can act as brakes. The energy they generate when braking is blown away as heat by powerful fans.

The Lectra Haul stands over five metres (16 ft) high, with a price tag to match. A new one costs around $900,000. Unlike long-distance haulers, the operating life of vehicles like this is calculated in total hours worked rather than distance traveled. Ten thousand hours of work is not unusual, even in the tough conditions of places like the vast copper mines of Zaire in Africa. In these mines, explosives experts blast out huge quantities at a time, enough to keep a team of dumpers busy for several days. The newly-mined rubble is carried away to be refined into high-grade ore, suitable for making into a wide variety of things, including copper pans and copper wire.

Big as the Lectra Haul is, it is outsized by another giant, the world's largest rigid two-axle truck, named "King of the Lode." This dump truck, with a cab 6.7 metres (22 ft) off the ground, was designed in the United States and built by the Australia-based firm of Wiseda. A fleet of Kings works in western Australia, hauling iron ore.

△ King of the Lode dump truck, compared in size with a family car. The dumper's name comes from its job in Australia, where a dump truck team carries away ore taken from a huge lodestone (iron ore) mine.

Construction vehicles

Here are three heavy-duty construction trucks. Vehicles like these are designed for a variety of building site jobs, including cement mixing, dumping and girder transport. Some of the biggest off-road vehicles stay there, as they are too big to go on any highway.

▽ The West German Faun company makes this six-axle crane carrier.

△ The construction of this Lectra Haul is as massive as the loads it carries. Steel up to 2.5 cm (1 in) thick is used. With its cargo bay full, the dump truck can move at about 18 km/h (11 mph) on rough terrain. Though this one is a two-axle rigid, there are also 6x6 dumpers and semi types with swiveling center-joints for good maneuverability.

◁ This Oshkosh 8x6 concrete mixer has a front-mounted chute, so the driver can see exactly where the load is going.

▽ The Terberg 8x8 has steering on all wheels. It is used for pipe and girder hauling and similar work.

Wreck and recovery

When vehicles crash or break down, that's when wreck and recovery crews go into action. Wrecker trucks have lifting machinery. Breakdown trucks carry much extra equipment, such as chains, cable, metal-cutting blow torches and so on. Recovery vehicles are used for towing jobs.

One of the pioneers of this type of work was Ernest Holmes, an American automobile repairman. His 1914 machine was the world's first powered twin-boom wrecker truck. The booms were small cranes that swung out from either side of the truck. While one was lifting a wrecked vehicle, the other could be hooked to a stout tree for extra support. Stabilizer legs could be lowered to give a firm base. Twin-boom wreckers are still popular for heavy-duty lifting work.

◁ Before the Holmes wrecker, vehicle recovery was very laborious. Here four soldiers dig a truck out of the mud of a World War I battlefield. Aboard their breakdown vehicle, they carried a metal lifting tripod, lengths of chain, rope and other useful equipment. All the lifting was done using muscle power.

◁ The 1914 Holmes twin-boom was the first motor wrecker, with lifting cables powered by the vehicle engine. On this rig, a pair of stabilizing legs dropped down from the two boom posts. Today's vehicles often have stabilizers extending outward, for a wider, more secure, working base.

Trucking colors

Truck paint schemes are rolling advertisements for the owners and the goods carried inside. Even factory-fresh trucks now come in bright colors.

△ This diagram shows how a twin-boom wrecker can be used for awkward rescues. Here, one boom and hook is used for lifting, the other secures the rig, preventing it from toppling over.

▽ The hooks from the booms of this wrecker are held in place by a metal crossbar when they are not in use. Powerful floodlights are used for illumination during night operations.

△ Drivers often like to personalize their trucks. This Isuzu, spotted in Thailand, is a good example.

▽ The enthusiastic driver of this DAF has added extra lights and a fringed curtain inside the driving cab.

Future trucks

Tomorrow's trucks will be designed for improved safety and fuel economy, with much less engine pollution.

Among the safety ideas from the German company Mercedes-Benz are such features as electronic tire pressure control and anti-skid systems. Rear-facing video cameras will give drivers a clear view when reversing and reduce the need for big mirrors. Truck bodies will be much more streamlined, inspired by the success of aerodynamic performance cars.

Manufacturers are also aiming to reduce the empty weight of their trucks. Less weight means less wear and tear on the roads, less vibration damage to bridges and buildings and better fuel consumption.

Diesel engines will include special cleaning equipment to reduce the pollution caused by smelly, black exhaust fumes. In fact, with efficient antipollution gear, diesels are likely to become the cleanest engines on the roads. And this, together with good fuel economy, will ensure that the diesel remains the main form of truck engine for the foreseeable future.

△ The cab includes a full range of electronic control systems.

▷ A vehicle like this could herald a new age of steam. The sleekly styled body design is based on a Japanese Nissan ATP-III truck project, while the engine comes from an experimental Mercedes-Benz 310 minibus which uses hydrogen as fuel. The waste product from the engine is nothing but water, in the form a steam exhaust.

🄷 Storage tank for hydrogen fuel

Supertruck pulls up with red container. Blue container awaits pickup.

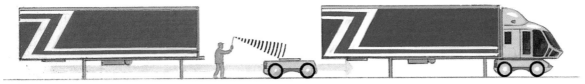

Red container legs fold down. Rear unit maneuvered under tail of blue container.

Driver shown to same scale as supertruck.

Supertruck, year 2010

This gleaming rig consists of three sections – a tractor, a streamlined container with detachable tail cone, and a rear wheel pod. The truck includes such features as a sleek plastic body, attached to a metal frame. Boarding steps extend from the cab like the stairs of a passenger jet. Inside the cab, the driver has a satellite telephone, a computer navigation unit and a steering system that uses digital controls like those used on modern airliners. Comforts include hi-fi sound and air conditioning.

The radical machine is based on some of the ideas of designer Adrian Tissington. Its tractor section is a 4x4 unit, for maximum grip in all conditions. Both tractor and tail units have antilock brakes for safe handling in wet weather. With this unit, jackknifing is a thing of the past. When parked, the container has drop-down legs to support it. The driver can then use a remote control to move the rear pod from under the container, using its own built-in electric motors. When it is positioned under a new container, the driver backs up the tractor to link up, then drives off in the complete rig.

Trucking progress

On these pages, you can see how trucks have developed, from the early days of road transport to today's supertrucks.

▷ **1911 Berliet.** Like other trucks of its day, this French truck was fired up by turning the crank handle below the radiator.

◁ **1924 Thornycroft Q-type.** One of the earliest semitrucks, the 1924 Thornycroft had wheels equipped with solid rubber tires.

▽ **1947 KB International.** This was an improved version of a semitruck that was designed before World War II.

▷ **1939 Fiat 626N.** Italy's popular three-ton Fiat truck served freight haulage companies and the Italian armed forces.

◁ **1953 GMC.** A typical long-distance hauler of the 1950s. It had a small sleeper compartment mounted directly behind the driver's cab.

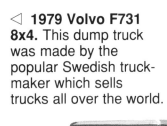

◁ **1979 Volvo F731 8x4.** This dump truck was made by the popular Swedish truck-maker which sells trucks all over the world.

▽ **1966 Mercedes-Benz LPS 1418.** This truck came from West Germany. Its nose was decorated with the distinctive Mercedes-Benz three-pointed star badge.

△ **1980s Leyland Roadtrain.** The Roadtrain had the advantage of many standard components, which could be used across a wide range of trucks.

▷ **1990s Renault AE500 Magnum.** This is one of Europe's supertrucks, with a high cab and smooth styling. Swing-out side panels reveal check points for oil and fuel.

27

Facts and records

Trucks have ranged from small, single seat electric delivery vehicles to giant diesel-powered monsters, which weigh 300 tons or more. Here you can read about some of these record breakers.

There are several contenders for the title of the world's first truck. Among the earliest were the 1892 steam vans made by Maurice LeBlant. These small vehicles had a driver in front to steer, and a stoker at the back to feed the furnace.

At the beginning of World War I, there were about 6,000 transport vehicles near the front line in France, ready to support the allied troops. By 1918, the number had grown to 92,000.

Though it is not a standard production machine, the Ford 9000 run by Ken Warby of the United States is probably the world's most powerful truck. Instead of a diesel engine, Warby's truck has an ex-air force J79 jet engine, mounted behind the cab. Warby has blasted down a 402m (quarter mile) straight in the Ford at 338 km/h (210 mph), a speed he reached in just 4.4 seconds. The Ford-J79 truck weighs in at nearly 4.5 tons.

The world's most powerful wrecking truck is a 1969 International M6-23. This wrecker has a lifting power of no less than 295 tons.

Truck companies sometimes think up weird ideas to promote their vehicles. One of the oddest is that of the Leyland firm, which employs a family of French stunt drivers to show off the trucks – driving them on their sides, on two wheels only. The record for such side-driving is held by Gilbert Bataille, who drove a Leyland T45 Road Runner on two wheels for a distance of 4.6 km (2.86 miles), during a truck race meeting at the Silverstone circuit in Britain.

Truck racing (shown in the photograph below) has become a popular sport in recent years. Drivers often pull up at meetings in their regular trucks, unhitch the trailer, and drive

◁ Under this Scania truck's cab is a powerful diesel engine, mounted low in the steel chassis.

Pollution control is a high priority for the Swedish firm of Scania. The latest Electronic Diesel Control (EDC) system uses computer technology to govern engine speed and the efficiency of oil burning in the engine. Another Scania project is to use ethanol, a clean-burning fuel obtained from plants. Noise limits are also a concern. The most likely method of reducing noise is to surround the engine with a "capsule" of sound-absorbing panels.

Many truckers have a "spy in the cab". This is the tachograph, a circular card recording system that shows how fast and for how long the truck is running. The aim of the tachograph is to ensure that drivers do not spend too long at the wheel, get tired, and possibly cause an accident.

straight on to the racing circuit. High tractor units corner surprisingly well, considering their bulk. They are helped by the fact that weight is concentrated at the bottom, in the engine and chassis units.

A "wheelie" on a motorcycle involves accelerating sharply, and lifting the front wheel off the ground. With enough power, you can do the same trick in a truck. In August 1987, stunt driver Steve Murty managed to wheelie his massive vehicle for 412.5 m (1,353 ft) at a showground in Ireland.

The biggest dump truck of all is the Terex Titan 33-19. Loaded up with rock and soil, it weighs in at 549 tons, of which 317 tons is cargo.

The largest dump truck tires are made by the Goodyear company. These giants measure 3.65 m (12 ft) across and weigh 5,670 kg (12,500 lb).

The longest truck is a staggering 174 m (572 ft) long. It was built for the U.S. Army for use in arctic regions such as Alaska. The Le Tourneau Arctic Snow Train, shown below, has 54 wheels, can run at up to 32 km/h (20 mph), and has a crew of six.

The biggest transport vehicles ever built are the two Marion crawlers that were built to transport Saturn V moon rockets to their launch pads at Cape Canaveral. The vehicles crawl on eight sets of caterpillar tracks, at the snail's pace of about 1.6 km/h (1 mph). Complete with rocket on top, each crawler weighs over 8,000 tons.

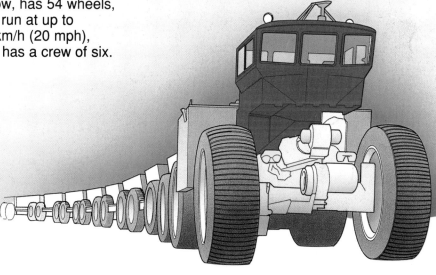

Truck technology

This glossary explains many of the technical terms used in this book.

Air drag
Resistance of the air, caused by objects pushing through it at speed. On highways, air drag accounts for much of the power needed for cruising. Smooth body styling helps reduce air drag, since the airflow is channeled over and away from the speeding truck.

Antilock Brake System (ABS)
Type of brake system that is designed to prevent wheels from skidding on slippery roads. Used on semitrucks, ABS is particularly useful to prevent jackknifing.

Container
Standard-size metal box, designed to fit on trucks, ships or trains. The advantage of a container is that once loaded, it need not be opened again until reaching its destination. On a single long journey, a container can be transferred from a truck to a ship or a train, quickly and easily using mobile cranes for the job.

Cab-over
Name used for a truck design in which the engine is mounted underneath the cab. This is also known as forward control,

because the steering system is mounted in front of the engine. By contrast, a conventional truck is one where the engine is mounted ahead of the driver's cab, under a long hood.

Chassis
Metal backbone of a truck, on which all the major components, including the engine, fuel tanks, wheels, suspension system and cab, are attached. The chassis structure is usually of thick, heavy-duty steel.

Diesel engine
The first diesel engine was built by German engineer Rudolf Diesel in 1897. It is an internal-combustion

engine that burns oil ignited by the heat resulting from high pressure in the cylinders. The diesel engine has several advantages over a gasoline engine. It is simple, needing no spark plug system. Diesel oil is cheaper than gas, and safer too, because it doesn't burn easily if spilled. And the diesel engine is much more economical than a gasoline engine.

Drive chain
Connection between the engine and wheels, often used by early trucks. Modern trucks use a metal driveshaft.

Hydrogen fuel
Experimental fuel which uses hydrogen gas,

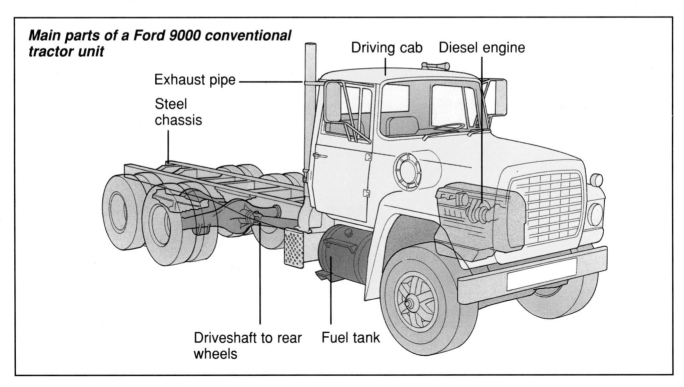

Main parts of a Ford 9000 conventional tractor unit

Driving cab · Diesel engine

Exhaust pipe

Steel chassis

Driveshaft to rear wheels · Fuel tank

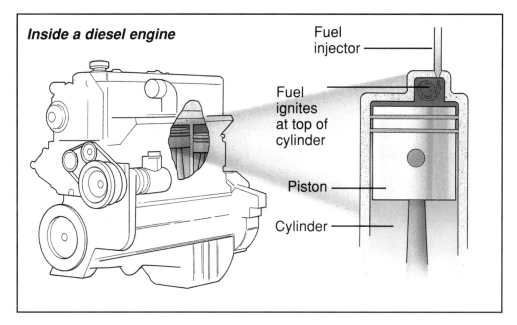

Inside a diesel engine

Fuel injector

Fuel ignites at top of cylinder

Piston

Cylinder

instead of gasoline or diesel oil. In a Mercedes-Benz design, the hydrogen is stored in special metal pellets, called hydrides, and the fuel is released slowly to the engine as required.

Internal combustion (IC) engine
General term for all engines that burn fuel inside the engine, rather than, for example, a steam engine which needs an outside furnace to provide heat. IC engines include both gasoline and diesel types.

Satellite communications

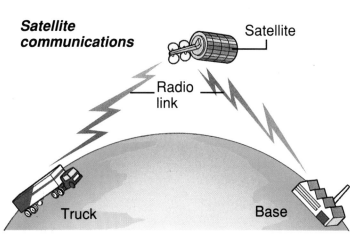

Satellite

Radio link

Truck

Base

Jackknife
When a semi vehicle skids out of control, the whole rig can split sideways, like a jackknife closing.

Modular construction
System that allows components to slot in and out of position easily, like building blocks. It allows for quick replacement of components if they go wrong.

Pneumatic tire
Air-filled tire, used on almost all road vehicles. The air in the tire helps to cushion

the ride. Before pneumatic tires came into general use, trucks came with metal or solid rubber tires.

Pollution
In the case of the diesel engine, the smoky exhaust gases contain various pollutants, including oxides of nitrogen (NOx), hydrocarbons (HC), carbon monoxide (CO) and solid particles in the form of black smoke. Various forms of pollution control equipment are under development, including devices called catalysts and exhaust traps.

Rig
General truckers' term for a complete truck that is ready to roll.

Rigid
Term used to describe any non-semi truck.

Roadtrain
Australian truck, which has several trailers and a huge amount of cargo, often three or

four times greater than the loads allowed in European countries.

Satellite radio
Long-distance communications system using a space satellite to link trucker and base. This means that drivers do not have to stop to make check-in calls. Also, the position of a truck can be pinpointed at any time.

Semi
A type of truck that comes in two sections. The tractor unit pulls a semitrailer carrying the load.

Semitrailer
The load-carrying section of an semi rig. Many semis have drop-down front legs so they can be parked while the tractor unit goes on another run.

Sleeper compartment
Small section behind or above the driving cab. It contains the driver's overnight accommodation.

Steamer
Term used for a steam-powered truck.

TIR
Letters that stand for the words Transports Internationaux Routiers. TIR is the system used by the long-distance truckers of Europe.

Tractor unit
Engine and driving cab section of a tractor/semitrailer rig.

Index

Africa 20
air drag 30
Alaska 29
"Anteater" 14
antilock brakes 11, 30
antipollution measures 24
anti-skid control 24
Australia 16, 20

Bataille, Gilbert 28
Benz, Karl 6
Berliet truck 26
"bulldog" see Mack
Burma 23

cab-over trucks 14, 30
Cape Canaveral 29
construction vehicles 20, 21
containers 4, 16, 25, 30
conventional trucks 14, 30
copper mine 20
Cugnot, Nicolas 4, 6
Cummins diesel engine 20

DAF trucks 9, 23
Daimler 5, 6
Dart trucks 18, 19
Darwin 16
diesel power 10, 24, 30, 31
Diesel, Rudolf 30

Edison nickel iron batteries 9
EDC systems 29
ethanol fuel 29
Europe 6, 16, 17, 27, 31

Faun trucks 21
Fiat 626N 26
Foden steamer 7

Ford 9000 28, 31
    Motor Company 19
France 8, 28
French Army 4

Germany 5, 12
GMC truck 27
Goodyear tyre company 29
Great Britain 9, 28
Gurney, Goldsworthy 6, 7

Holland 9
Holmes, Ernest 22
Holmes wrecker 22
hydrogen fuel 24, 31

intercontinental trucks 4
internal-combustion engine 6, 30, 31
International M6-23 28
Ireland 29
Isuzu truck 23
Iveco-Ford Turbostar 5

J79 jet engine 28
jackknifing 11, 25, 30, 31
Japan 18

KB International 26
Kenworth T600
    Aerodyne 14
    tractor-trailer rig 19
"King of the Lode" 20

Langert wagon 6
Leaping Lena 18
LeBlant, Maurice 28
Lectra Haul M100 20, 21
Le Tourneau Arctic Snow Train 29
Leyland trucks 9, 28
    Roadtrain 27
    T45 Road Runner 28

lodestone mine 20
Mack AC "bulldog" 8
Marion crawlers 29
Mercedes-Benz
    310 minibus 24,30
    company 24
    LPS 1418 27
Mexico 18
military trucks 12, 13
Minuteman missile carrier 12
modular construction 13, 31
Murty, Steve 29

Nissan ATP-III 24

off-road driving 12
Oshkosh 8x6 21
Otto, Nicolaus 6

Pegaso 5
Philadelphia 6
pollution control 31

Renault AE500
Magnum 27
Reo semitanker 12
rigid trucks 10, 11, 31
roadtrains 16, 31
"roo bars" 16

satellite communications systems 14, 25, 31
Saturn V moon rockets 29
Scammell trucks 18
    Pioneer 10
Scania truck company 29
semitrailers 11, 14, 30, 31
semitrucks 10, 11, 12, 14, 26, 30, 31
Silverstone circuit 28
sleeper cabs 14, 26, 31
Space Shuttle Orbiter 19

"spy in the cab" 29
Spain 5
steamers, steam trucks 4, 6, 7, 31
steam traction engines 7
steam vans 28
Sydney 16

tachograph see "spy in the cab"
tank transporters 13
Terberg 8x8 20
Terex Titan 33-19 29
Thornycroft steamer 7
    Q-type 26
TIR trucks 16, 17, 31
tires 8, 9, 31
Tissington, Adrian 25
truck badges '9
    chassis 30
    colors 23
    costs 14
    racing 28

United States 6, 10, 14, 15, 16, 20, 28, 29
U.S. Army 29

Volvo trucks 17
    F731 8x4 27

Walker electric truck 8
Warby, Ken 28
West Germany 27
wheel code system 13
"wheelie" 29
White artic 11
White Freightliner 15
Wiseda 20
World War I 8, 9, 10, 22, 28
World War II 12, 26
wreck and recovery trucks 22, 23, 28

Zaire 20

PRINTED IN BELGIUM BY

proost
INTERNATIONAL BOOK PRODUCTION